HORSES
AND PONIES

Consultant:
G. Alexander
of the United States Polo Association

Photo Credits:

Kendra Bond—Pages 9, 13, 14-15
Kent & Donna Dannen—Pages 10, 11, 20, 22
Carrie Fink—Page 16
Ron Kimball—Cover; Pages 8, 15
Dwight Kuhn—Pages 14, 14-15, 15
Zig Leszczynski—Page 24
Don & Pat Valenti—Pages 20-21, 27
Brian Bahr/Allsport—Page 29
Vandystandt/Allsport—Page 20
Corbis-Bettman—Pages 16, 17, 18
Tom Beakefiled/DRK—Page 7
Tom Bean/DRK—Pages 25, 28
Melinda Berge/DRK—Pages 18-19, 19
N.H. Cheatham/DRK—Page 28
Chuck Dresner/DRK—Page 15
Thomas Dressler/DRK—Page 7
James R. Fisher/DRK—Page 20
C.C. Lockwood/DRK—Page 9
Andy Rouse/DRK—Page 9
Barbara Cushaan Rowel/DRK—Page 23
Jeremy Woodhouse/DRK—Pages 22-23
Porter Gifford/Gamma-Liason—Pages 8-9, 27
Daniel Simon/Gamma-Liason—Page 28
The Granger Collection—Pages 18, 22
Lindsay Silverman/International Stock—Page 29
Daniel Aubry/Liason International—Page 6
J. Eastcott & Y. Momatiuk/Masterfile—Pages 6-7, 19, 24-25, 26, 27
Tim Fitzharris/Masterfile—Pages 12-13
Courtney Milne/Masterfile—Page 10
Cameron Read/Masterfile—Page 11
Shooting Star—Page 21
F. Chehu/Vandystandt—Page 14
Richard Martin/Vandystandt—Page 20-21
D. Cavagnaro/Visuals Unlimited—Page 6
A.J. Copley/Visuals Unlimited—Page 6
Mark E. Gibson/Visuals Unlimitied—Page 28
Jeff Greenberg/Visuals Unlimited—Page 27
Linda H. Hopsow/Visuals Unlimited—Page 12
Jane McAlonan/Visuals Unlimited—Page 10-11
Joe McDonald/Visuals Unlimited—Page 7
Jo Prater/Visuals Unlimited—Page 16-17
Kjell B. Sandved/Visuals Unlimited—Page 25
John Sohlden/Visuals Unlimited—Page 13
Bernd Wittich/Visuals Unlimited—Page 11
Visuals Unlimited—Page 23

Copyright © 1997
Kidsbooks, Inc.
3535 West Peterson Ave.
Chicago, IL 60659

Visit us at www.kidsbooks.com
Volume discounts available for group purchases.

EYES ON NATURE™

HORSES AND PONIES

Written by
Donald Olson

kidsbooks®
Incorporated

HORSE STORY

THE FIRST HORSE

Horses of today come from a small mammal called Eohippus (E-O-hip-us) that was no larger than a fox. Eohippus had four toes on its front feet and three on the hind feet. Over millions of years, as Eohippus evolved, its legs grew longer and its toes developed into a single hoof. Now called Equus, the first modern horse looked more like a pony.

What is the only animal that can run for miles and leap over fences carrying a rider on its back? A horse, of course. Over the centuries horses have helped humans more than any other animal.

FOLLOW THE LEADER

Herd-dwelling animals, horses live in large groups with clearly defined social relationships. The females form mare groups, led by one senior female and one dominant male, or stallion. The status of the other mares depends on their age and strength.

PONY VS. HORSE

Ponies are technically horses, but they are much smaller and have a different character. The Shetland is the smallest pony, measuring four feet to the shoulder. The tallest horse, the shire, can be more than six feet in height.

THE HORSE FAMILY

The Equidae (E-kwid-e) family consists of horses, zebras, and asses. The Equidae are called "odd-toed" animals because they have only one hard hoof on each foot. The hoof makes it posible to run fast over long distances enabling them to escape from predators.

PUT UP YOUR DUKES ▼

When forced to protect themselves and their babies, or when they are fighting for dominance within the herd, horses can be fierce and dangerous. They will kick with their hind legs, strike with their front hooves, and bite. But when frightened, their instinct is to run.

▲ The onager was known in biblical times as the wild ass.

FINE FEATURES

A horse has many extraordinary features which allows it to have panoramic vision, the ability to sense oncoming storms, and to sleep standing up.

Mane

Shoulder

Loins

Back

Forelock

Croup

Withers

Muzzle

Tail

Neck

Chest

Hock

Stifle Belly

Forearm

Barrel

Elbow

Knee

Cannon Bone

Hoof

Fetlock

SNIFFING AROUND

In addition to increasing the air intake of a running horse, large nostrils allow for a sharp sense of smell. The horse familiarizes itself with other horses, humans, and objects by close-up sniffing.

When horses sniff one another, they are determining social standing in the herd.

COUNTING SHEEP

Horses spend about four hours per day, at half hour intervals, sleeping. Because they were often preyed upon in their original habitat, and needed to take flight on short notice—today, light sleeping in a standing position is not uncommon. However, horses need to lie in a dry, comfortable space to get deep, restful sleep.

8

PANORAMIC VISION

Because a horse's eyes are on opposite sides of its head, it has a larger field of vision than a human. As it grazes, a horse can see both sides of a field without focusing on any one thing. When a horse hears or smells something unusual, it can instantly sharpen its focus.

HEAR THAT?

With ears that swivel like antennas, a horse can pick up sounds from all directions. The position of a horse's ears also indicates mood. If the ears point back, the horse is angry or frightened; if one ear is pointing back and the other forward, the horse is uncertain.

NEIGH SPEAK

The language of horses speaks for itself. A neigh or a whinny is a call to horses in the distance. If there is a reply, it means a horse is nearby. A knicker, which sounds like a soft neigh, is given to a friend and becomes stronger if the horse is expecting food. A squeal is an expression of pain or playfullness.

SMILE

The area around a horse's nose, lips, and mouth is called the muzzle. Behind the muzzle are its long jaws, usually containing 40 teeth. The horse chews by moving its jaws from side to side. The age of a horse can be told by looking at its teeth— the older the horse, the more worn- down and discolored they are.

PONY TALES

Although they look similar, ponies are different from horses. Ponies usually grow no higher than 58 inches, yet they are sturdier on their feet than the horse.

THE OLD ONES

Some experts believe that all modern ponies developed from two ancient ponies. One is thought to have inhabited northwestern Europe, where it developed a resistance to harsh, wet conditions. The other, more heavily built, lived near Russia where it developed a resistance to cold. This theory may explain why ponies are such rugged creatures.

MR. TOUGH GUY

A tough pony, the Bashkir is an all-purpose working animal. Originally from the mountains near Siberia, it lives outside year-round, even in sub-zero temperatures, and is able to find food under deep snow. The winter coat of the Bashkir is so thick that the hair is some-times spun into cloth.

◄ PURE PONY

Though it's called a horse, the small Icelandic horse is really a pony. It has not been crossbred with any other horses for more than 1,000 years—making it the purest pony breed in existence.

ARMY RECRUIT

Considered to be one of the most beautiful ponies, the Welsh pony was used in the army to haul guns and equipment. In the city, the Welsh pony was in great demand with dairies and bakeries for carting goods.

▼ The Shetland (left) and Welsh ponies graze peacefully.

MOOR PONIES

The wild moorlands of southern England produced two breeds of ponies. The Exmoor is independent and still lives semi-wild. Over the centuries, the Dartmoor has been bred with Arabians, Welsh, and Thoroughbred horses, so there are few purebred Dartmoor ponies today.

▼ A Dartmoor pony mare with her foal.

MINIATURE HORSES

Miniature horses are not ponies. This distinctive breed of horse averages 30 inches in height to the shoulder. Its smaller size is a natural adaptation to severe climatic conditions and scarce food. Known to be good tempered and friendly, miniature horses have also been bred as pets.

TO THE CIRCUS

One of the world's strongest ponies, the Shetland can carry a person over rough countryside, pull heavy farm loads, and work in coal mines. It is also a popular circus performer.

11

SIZING THEM UP

Horses are divided into three groups that indicate where the breed originated.

DESERT GRAZERS

The Arabian and barb breeds, called *hotbloods*, originated in desertlike conditions where grazing lands were poor. As a result, hotbloods are lighter and faster than coldbloods, and have thin coats to help keep them cool.

◀ The Arabian horse breed.

The thoroughbred, derived from the Arabian and barb, can gallop at more than 40 miles per hour.

▲ HEAVY

Many *coldbloods* are large, heavy horses from cold climates. To survive freezing winters, these slow-moving horses developed thick skins and a layer of fat. Strength, rather than speed, is the hallmark of a coldblood. The biggest breed of horse in the world, the coldblooded British Shire, reaches six feet at the shoulder and weighs up to 2,900 pounds.

HOT & COLD

Crossing a hotblood with a coldblood produces a *warmblood.* Because they carry characteristics of both hotbloods and coldbloods, these horses are popular in competitive events.

This Hanoverian is practicing for an event called dressage (dre-sazh), which is a competitive sport and art form.

◀ The "leopard" is one of five distinctive coat patterns recognized in the apaloosa.

▼ COLOR COATING

Horses come in a variety of colors. One of the most beautiful horse colors is palomino. The coat is gold but the mane and tail are white. Unlike most horses, which are classified by breed, palominos are cross-registered for their breed and color.

WHO'S WHO?

Facial markings are recorded by horse breeders and used as a means of identification. A "star" is a small white shape on a horse's forehead, a "blaze" is a broad white stripe running down its snout, and a "snip" is a white patch between its nostrils.

This horse has a star and a snip.

13

FIRST STEPS

Amazingly, the baby horse, or foal, tries to stand on its wobbly legs within an hour after birth. Once on its feet, it tries to find its mother's nipples and begin nursing. A foal will nurse for about a year, but it will begin grazing after a few weeks.

THE FOLKS

An adult female horse is called a mare, and an adult male horse is called a stallion. Mares reach adulthood between their first and second years. Mares and stallions mate during the spring—a time when, in the wild, food is more plentiful.

A foal learns that it must keep up with its mother.

MOTHER KNOWS BEST

The mare is generally the foal's sole teacher and their bond is very close. Before it even knows how to eat grass, a week-old foal will imitate its mother's grazing posture.

FOALING AROUND

A female foal is called a filly, a male foal is called a colt. As they grow, colts and fillies love to play. They nip one another and kick up their legs. Running together teaches foals about survival behavior.

14

NAP TIME

A foal, like all babies, needs plenty of rest.
It will frequently lie down and nap.
But at the first sign of danger, it
quickly gets to its feet and runs
to its mother's side.

▼ This Clydesdale foal may
weigh up to one ton when
it is fully grown.

▲ An Arabian
mare nursing
her foal.

ALL GROWN UP

Weaning is when a foal learns to separate
itself from its mother. Domesticated foals are
generally weaned between four and six
months, and slightly later in the wild. The
weaned horse is called a weanling until it is
one year old, when it becomes a yearling.

By the time it is three years old this
bay yearling colt will reach its adult size.

15

This cave painting of a horse is probably 15,000 years old.

HORSE IN TIME

Of all domesticated animals, the horse was the last to be tamed by humans. Long before that happened, early peoples hunted horses for food and their sturdy hide.

The ancient Greeks and Romans used horses for chariot racing, which was first staged at the Olympic Games in 680 B.C.

CHARIOTS

The domestication of the horse was one of the most important events in human civilization. Horses made it easier to travel greater distances. Before they were ever ridden, horses and donkeys were trained to pull carts and chariots.

MYTHICAL HORSES

From earliest times, horses have inspired many fables. The centaur was half-human and half-horse. The unicorn had the body of a horse and one long horn on its head. Pegasus—a beautiful white horse with wings—was tamed by the Greek hero Bellerophon.

COURAGE UNDER FIRE

Some horses have become as renowned for their courage as their famous riders. Legend has it that Bucephalus, a wild horse belonging to the conquerer Alexander the Great (356-323 B.C.), would only respond to the commands of his master. When Bucephalus died, Alexander the Great built a town and monument and named it Bucephala in honor of his beloved horse.

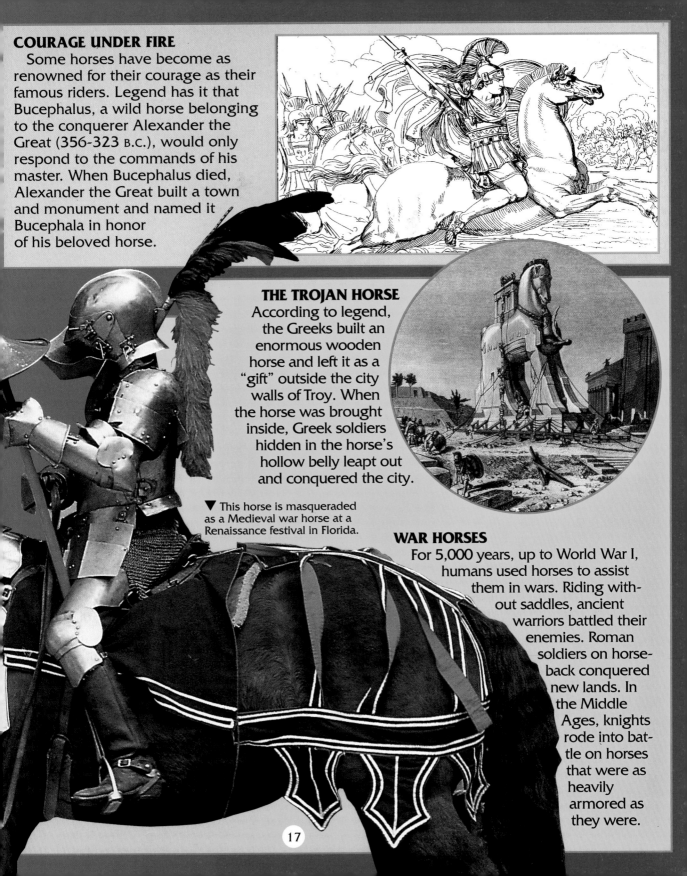

THE TROJAN HORSE

According to legend, the Greeks built an enormous wooden horse and left it as a "gift" outside the city walls of Troy. When the horse was brought inside, Greek soldiers hidden in the horse's hollow belly leapt out and conquered the city.

▼ This horse is masqueraded as a Medieval war horse at a Renaissance festival in Florida.

WAR HORSES

For 5,000 years, up to World War I, humans used horses to assist them in wars. Riding without saddles, ancient warriors battled their enemies. Roman soldiers on horseback conquered new lands. In the Middle Ages, knights rode into battle on horses that were as heavily armored as they were.

17

AMERICAN INDIANS ▲

At first, Native Americans were terrified of horses. But within 200 years, horses had become an essential part of Native American life. Horses simplified hunting and moving camp. And, as their enemies discovered, Indian warriors on horseback were dangerous foes.

REVOLUTIONARIES ▲

Horses played a large part in helping America gain independence from England. George Washington led his American troops on horseback. And Paul Revere raced from Boston to Concord on horseback to warn the colonists that the British were coming.

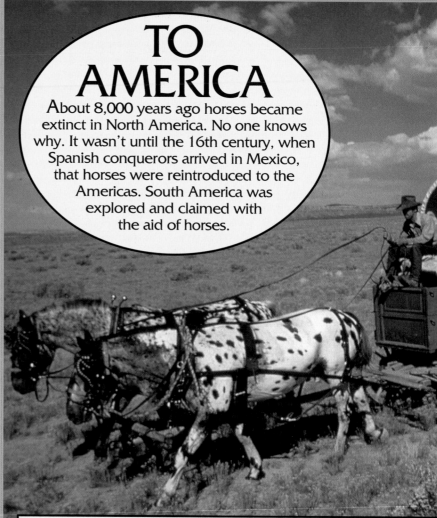

TO AMERICA

About 8,000 years ago horses became extinct in North America. No one knows why. It wasn't until the 16th century, when Spanish conquerors arrived in Mexico, that horses were reintroduced to the Americas. South America was explored and claimed with the aid of horses.

WESTWARD HO!

In the mid-19th century, thousands of Americans headed west seeking more land and better lives. Wagon trains, pulled by horses or mules, made the trek across the plains and over the Rocky Mountains. The trip took months, and many settlers and horses did not survive the hardships.

◀ TAXI!

Carts and coaches harnessed to horses rattled along the dirt roads of early America, moving people and goods from one place to another. In the winter, horses with jingling bells pulled sleighs through the snowy countryside. Horsedrawn buses moved down bustling city streets. As America grew, so did the use of horses.

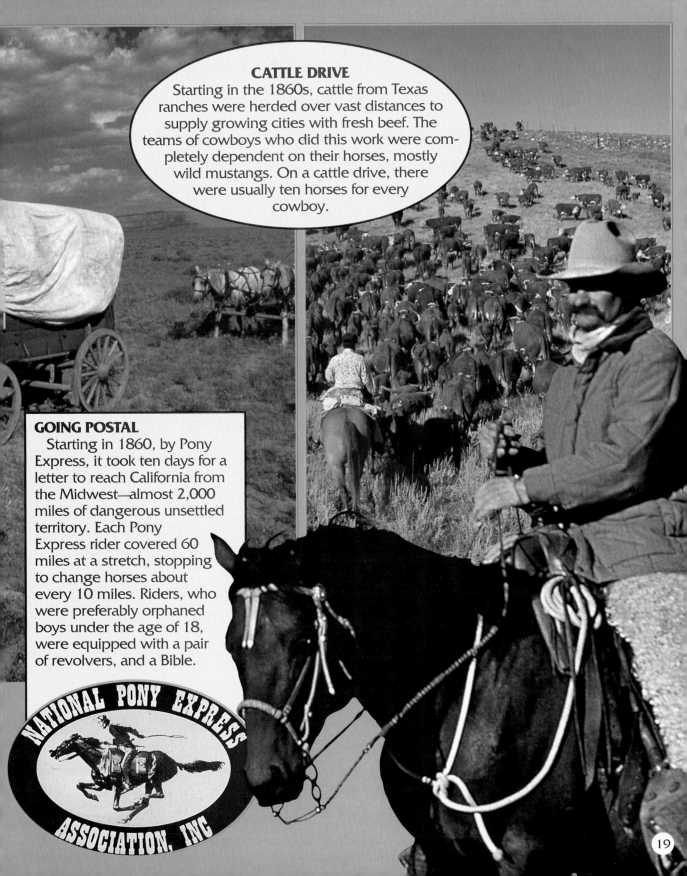

CATTLE DRIVE

Starting in the 1860s, cattle from Texas ranches were herded over vast distances to supply growing cities with fresh beef. The teams of cowboys who did this work were completely dependent on their horses, mostly wild mustangs. On a cattle drive, there were usually ten horses for every cowboy.

GOING POSTAL

Starting in 1860, by Pony Express, it took ten days for a letter to reach California from the Midwest—almost 2,000 miles of dangerous unsettled territory. Each Pony Express rider covered 60 miles at a stretch, stopping to change horses about every 10 miles. Riders, who were preferably orphaned boys under the age of 18, were equipped with a pair of revolvers, and a Bible.

NATIONAL PONY EXPRESS ASSOCIATION, INC

SHOW AND SPORT

Organized races on horseback were once popular with the ancient Greeks and Romans. Called "the sport of kings," horse racing now takes place at famous courses around the world.

◀ LEAPS AND BOUNDS

The steeplechase, a more dramatic form of horse racing, began in 18th-century England. The goal was to reach a distant landmark—usually a church steeple—by galloping across open fields and leaping over fences and hedges along the way.

▼ Lipizzaners are most often used for classical riding events.

◀ LET'S DANCE

Classical riding is a competitive system of horse training that dates back hundreds of years. The most difficult movements include one in which the horse trots in place with high, springy steps, and one where the horse spins in a tiny circle, its hind legs staying almost on the same spot.

A ▶ REAL EVENT

Horse trials, known as eventing, are the most difficult and demanding of all riding competitions. Eventing tests the endurance, speed, and skill of both horse and rider in three separate categories: dressage, which tests the ability of a horse to perform very difficult tricks, cross-country racing, and show jumping.

DESERT GAMES

One of the world's most spectacular horse festivals, fantasia, takes place in Morocco, on the fringes of the Sahara Desert. In a fantasia, a line of riders charge straight ahead until a signal is given by the leader. Then the riders stand up in their stirrups, bring their horses to an abrupt stop, and fire rifles into the air.

MOVIE-MARE

Our fascination with horses continues today in books, movies, and television. The Lone Ranger, with his trusty horse Silver, and sidekick Tonto, with his horse, Scout—a pinto—were a heroic team of wild-West crime fighters on 1950s television.

HORSE HOCKEY

Polo is one of the fastest games in the world. Riding at full gallop, two teams, each with four riders, use bamboo mallets to hit a ball through a goal post.

WORKING 9 TO 5

Today we don't see many horses in the cities where we live. But up until a hundred years ago, you would have seen them on the streets every day. Before there were cars or buses, light draft horses such as the Welsh Cob and the Cleveland Bay were harnessed to carriages and carried people around the city.

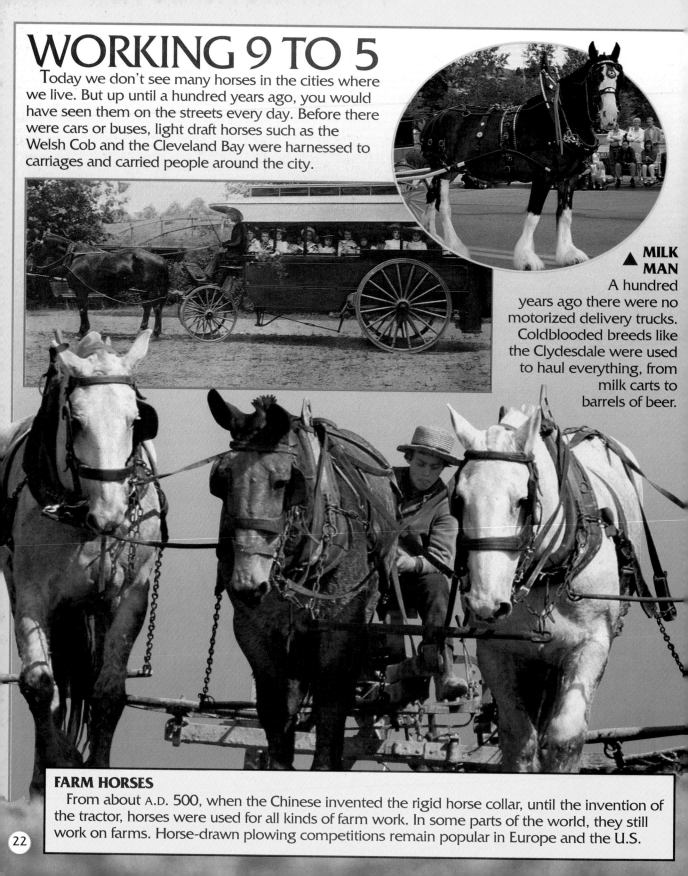

▲ MILK MAN

A hundred years ago there were no motorized delivery trucks. Coldblooded breeds like the Clydesdale were used to haul everything, from milk carts to barrels of beer.

FARM HORSES

From about A.D. 500, when the Chinese invented the rigid horse collar, until the invention of the tractor, horses were used for all kinds of farm work. In some parts of the world, they still work on farms. Horse-drawn plowing competitions remain popular in Europe and the U.S.

DONKEY WORK

With little nourishment, donkeys are able to carry heavy loads over long distances. Strong and surefooted, they were the first members of the horse family to be domesticated and have been used as pack and riding animals for thousands of years. In many parts of the world, donkeys are still used for hauling loads.

HORSE POWER

In factories, horses provided the power needed to keep engines and machines of all kinds running. Their work gave us the word "horsepower," a term used to measure the power of an engine.

FIRE FIGHTERS

Think of it—in the days before fire trucks, fire engines were pulled by three large horses. Once the alarm sounded, harnesses slid onto the horses' back from overhead frames, firemen fastened them up, and the entire rig was ready to roll in three to five minutes.

THE PITS

Pity the poor pit pony—he had one of the worst horse jobs of all. From the 19th century up until a few years ago, thousands of ponies spent their lives underground, working in the British coal mines.

HOW WILD IS WILD?

Sadly, there are no truly wild horses—horses that have never been domesticated by humans—living in the world today. Loss of habitat has taken its toll. The horses we call "wild" are more correctly called "feral." This means that they are descended from domesticated stock but are no longer under human control.

WILD MUSTANGS

More than 400 years ago the Spanish brought horses to North America. Some of those strong, fast-running Spanish horses escaped, multiplied, and formed the mustang herds that still roam remote parts of the American West. Once hunted almost to extinction, mustangs are now protected by law.

◀ Corralled feral horses.

▲ A VANISHED BREED

The last herd of truly wild horses was discovered in 1881 in a remote mountain area on the edge of the Gobi Desert in Mongolia. These fierce horses, called Przewalski's horse, are sandy in color and have stiff, upright manes.

THE WILD WEST

The largest herds of wild horses in the U.S. are found in the Owyhee Desert of northern Nevada. Roaming over vast areas in search of food and water, the animals are attracted to this area by lush early-summer grasses.

MAKING A SPLASH ▲

Camargues are a special breed of white, wild horses that have lived in the saltwater marshes of the Rhone delta in southern France for thousands of years. Their wide hooves make it easier to move on soft wet grasslands and reach the coarse reeds they use for food.

SWIMMING PONIES

On two islands off the coast of Virginia, there lives a special herd of about 200 scrubby-looking ponies called Chincoteague ponies. Every year, they are rounded up for an auction where the foals are selected and sold.

THE HUMAN TOUCH

Most horses and ponies today are raised by humans. They are accustomed to handling and the routines of a stable. But horses are not, by nature, domestic animals. They adapt themselves to human ways because they have the ability to do so. If properly treated and cared for, a horse will form a close and affectionate bond with its human handler.

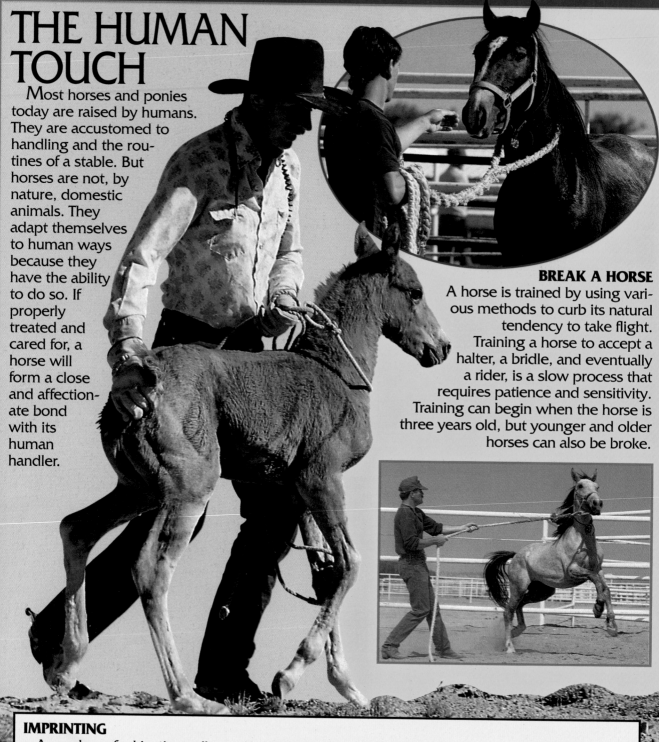

BREAK A HORSE

A horse is trained by using various methods to curb its natural tendency to take flight. Training a horse to accept a halter, a bridle, and eventually a rider, is a slow process that requires patience and sensitivity. Training can begin when the horse is three years old, but younger and older horses can also be broke.

IMPRINTING

A newborn foal instinctually attaches itself to, and follows, whatever is looming above it. Normally, this is its protective mother. Some horse owners now use a technique called "imprinting" to bond with foals immediately after birth. When it is held and rubbed by its human handler, a newborn foal learns not to run away or be afraid.

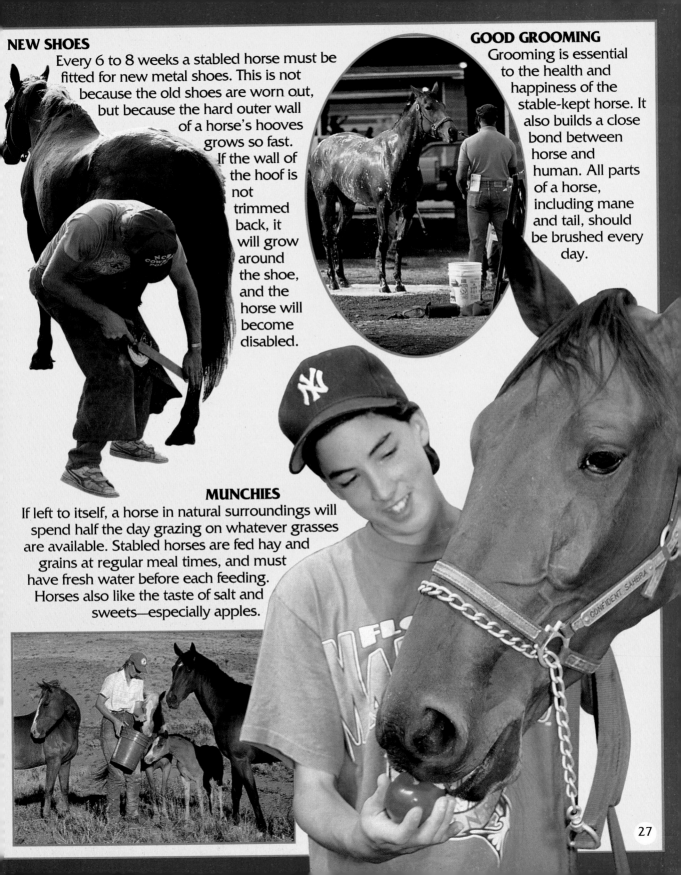

NEW SHOES

Every 6 to 8 weeks a stabled horse must be fitted for new metal shoes. This is not because the old shoes are worn out, but because the hard outer wall of a horse's hooves grows so fast. If the wall of the hoof is not trimmed back, it will grow around the shoe, and the horse will become disabled.

GOOD GROOMING

Grooming is essential to the health and happiness of the stable-kept horse. It also builds a close bond between horse and human. All parts of a horse, including mane and tail, should be brushed every day.

MUNCHIES

If left to itself, a horse in natural surroundings will spend half the day grazing on whatever grasses are available. Stabled horses are fed hay and grains at regular meal times, and must have fresh water before each feeding. Horses also like the taste of salt and sweets—especially apples.

27

HORSES TODAY

Although we do not rely on horses as much as before the invention of the motor, horses are still an essential part of modern life. Horses and ponies are still used for farm-work and to carry loads in many countries, and they have been part of parades and pageantry for centuries.

GIDDAP

A riding stable is a good place to learn about horses. Horseback riding is fun, and stables with gentle, well-trained horses are found all over the U.S.

TREKKING

Horses and ponies are used in treks through the wilderness, helping people visit remote areas inaccessible by car. It would be impossible for a human to carry supplies to the bottom of the Grand Canyon.

▲ A performance by Canadian mounties.

MOUNTED POLICE

Mounted police are found in cities throughout the world. Their job is to patrol crowds, parks, and public spaces.

▲ CAROUSELS

At one time, almost everyone knew how to ride a horse. Maybe that's why merry-go-rounds are so popular. Riding on a carousel horse reminds us of how important these beautiful animals once were in our everyday lives.

KENTUCKY HORSE PARK

The state of Kentucky is famous for its horses, and pays tribute to them at the Kentucky Horse Park. More than 40 different horse and pony breeds, including some world champions, can be seen in the park's stables. There are also special horse museums, a race track, polo grounds, and tours in horse-drawn carriages.

▲ RODEOS

Rodeos test the skills developed by cowboys in the early days of cattle ranching. They are uniquely American events. Calf roping and saddle bronc riding are classic rodeo events. In bronc riding, riders can use only one hand and must stay on the bucking bronco for eight seconds.